I Learn to Love My Enemies

Carolyn Nystrom

Illustrated by
Dwight Walles

MOODY PRESS
CHICAGO

Moody Press, a ministry of the Moody Bible Institute, is designed for education,
evangelization, and edification. If we may assist you
in knowing more about Christ and the Christian Life,
please write us without obligation:
Moody Press, c/o MLM, Chicago, Il 60610

ISBN: 0-8024-6174-3

Printed in the United States of America

1 2 3 4 5 6 7 8 Printing/DP/Year 94 93 92 91 90

"Shelly and Abbie, if I see one more fistful of sand in the air, I'm going to separate you for a whole week!" Mom yelled from the back door.

I opened my hand slowly and let the wet stuff fall into our sand pit. Abbie's hair was matted with wet sand. A glob of it clung to her shoulder. She even had wet sand smeared down her cheek. And I'd put it all there. Abbie glared at me, nodded at my empty hand, and turned her back.

The summer afternoon had started happily enough. The day was hot and sticky. So we asked Mom if we could use the garden hose to fill our sand pit with water. Cool sandy water squished between our toes, while hot sun warmed our backs. We made tunnels and castles and islands and mountains and rivers and roads and bridges. We even pretended that the wet sand was snow— and Abbie made a snowman and planted him on an island. We laughed at his silly grin.

Then the hose slipped in Abbie's hand, and she got my hair wet. And her foot slipped in the water, and she stepped on my castle. And I felt anger creeping up the back of my neck like a prickly lizard. I felt my fist crush the silly snowman and fling the sand at Abbie while she howled that I was wrecking her island.

Now it looked like I might have to spend a whole week without my best friend. Even though I was mad at her, I knew that a week without Abbie would be a long lonely week.

Abbie and I decided that
day that we were too hot and
tired to play any longer in the
sand. We remembered to
turn off the hose, which
made Mom a little happier.

We also remembered to brush the sand off our bodies, which helped matters too. Then we went into the house to read books. Abbie likes to draw, and I like to read, so I read out loud to her while she drew pictures of the stories. Then I got tired of trying to puzzle out strange words, so I made up stories and told them to Abbie while she drew. The stories got sillier and sillier. Pretty soon we were laughing and rolling on the floor.

Luke 6:31

"Hey, that's just what we did!" I shouted. "The sun was bright and hot when we stopped fighting in the sandpile. And when evening came we were friends again."

"I'm glad you did it that way," Mom said. "What did you do that helped you get over being angry?"

took off my sweatshirt and hung it on our lilac bush. Then Abbie and I climbed on the teeter-totter. Just then we saw Jennifer coming up our driveway. She stood for a minute and watched us.

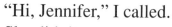
Luke 6: 27-30

"Hi, Jennifer," I called.
She didn't answer.
"Do you want to play?" I said slowly.
I hoped she'd say no. But she didn't say
anything at all. Jennifer just stood there
watching us and making marks in the dirt
with the toe of her boot.

Will Jennifer ever become our friend? Will I ever get my sweatshirt and sand pail back? I don't know. Maybe not. But I can pray for Jennifer. And I can be kind to her. I can do that because God is kind to me. And God gave me a lot more than a pail and a sweatshirt. God gave me the best gift of all. God gave me Jesus.